THO
A I

Introduction

Thomas Merton is one of the most famous American Catholic authors of the twentieth century. A prolific author, Merton published thirty-six books and collections of poems while he was alive over the span of twenty-seven years, and has thirty-eight posthumous publications that bear his name. Even more impressive than his voluminous output, however, is his deep spirituality that enraptured generations of people seeking intimate union with God. Overflowing with sincerity, profundity, and humility, his works have inspired many people to seek the face of God. Merton's life is a beautiful testimony of a soul who yearned for God and, moreover, sought him in the context of twentieth century America. For this reason, and on account of the quality of Merton's own writings, especially of The Seven Storey Mountain, his autobiography written at the age of 33, Merton has been a popular spiritual author for over half a century not just in America, but the world over, where his autobiography has been translated into over twenty languages.

This is the story of a man who sought God throughout his life and dedicated himself to a life of holiness. Despite his magnetic personality, his quest for God, and his life as an ascetic Trappist monk, there are some who disparage Merton, claiming that he is responsible for watering down the truth of the Catholic faith by dialoguing with religions of the East, in particular Zen Buddhism, toward the end of his life. How can it be, they wonder, that this man, who wrote so profoundly of the mystical union of God, can abandon the firmness of his faith and seek other gods as Solomon of old abandoned his wisdom to worship the foreign gods of his many wives?

What complicates matters more is that Merton had a relationship with a young nurse toward the end of his life, one that he describes as an affair although he never technically slept with her. There is no beating around the bush that this is a scandalous episode in Merton's life, but for one to condemn Merton and his thought outright for this moral lapse is premature and sanctimonious; after all, Jesus himself said to those who were ready to stone the woman caught in the act of adultery, "Let he who is without sin cast the first stone." None of us can claim to be sinless.

Two Mertons seem to emerge from this debate: one that was faithful to God through his life from his entrance into the Trappist monastery onward, and another that went further and further astray toward the end of his life. Which of these Mertons is the real Merton? In terms of his fidelity to God, this is something that only God really knows. What we are able to do in this explication of Merton's life is explain the major episodes in Merton's life and provide an explanation as to what makes him a unique and relevant spiritual voice for today.

This book is an attempt to understand the mystery of Merton, a man who was himself familiar with mystery. It is a biography that seeks to know who Merton was and the path that he followed, and seeks to determine insofar as possible whether he was faithful to that path. It is not my purpose to definitively judge one way or another; instead, I seek to explain how Merton's journey can be interpreted as a faithful attempt to live out a Christian life. This is different from determining that he was absolutely faithful or was a complete failure.

There are many captivating settings to this story: the culture-steeped villages of France, the ancient halls of Cambridge in England, the church studded surroundings of ancient Rome, the sprawling urban excitement of New York, the quaint, silent, and solemn Trappist Monastery in Kentucky, and the exotic lands of the Orient. These settings show the cosmopolitan nature of Thomas Merton and bring the reader into close contact with these distant lands.

I am indebted to Merton's The Seven Storey Mountain for information about his early life. Although pouring through Merton's thick autobiography (some versions are around 500 pages long) to distill the highlights of his early life poses some challenges, it is rewarding. After this book, I especially found helpful Michael W. Higgins's Thomas Merton: Faithful Visionary.

Although this book does not purport to be an academic exposition of Merton's life and work, it will hopefully shed some light on Thomas Merton for people who are familiar with his work and for those who are new to Merton. Ideally, it will lead to a greater acceptance of Merton's merit in an age that tends to be hypercritical and overzealous, especially concerning people or ideas that are unfamiliar. Powerful witnesses to God are rare in this day and age, so it is important that Merton gets a fair hearing. It is my conviction that although Merton has his share of critics, his life is worth examining and has elements in it that are capable of inspiring many people today.

Infancy in France and Childhood in New York

Thomas Merton was born on January 31, 1915 in Prades, France to two artists, Owen Merton, from New Zealand, and Ruth Jenkins, from the United States. Merton's parents each had different religious preferences: while his mother gravitated toward Quakerism, his father had ties to the Church of England. No one could have predicted that the son of these two people would have become a great Catholic mystic. The circumstances of Merton's own existence are seen as quite providential from two considerations. First, Merton recounts how his father, while still in New Zealand, was seriously considering going on an expedition to the South Pole, but ultimately decided against it. This was fortunate for Merton since he would not have been born; no one from the expedition ever returned. Second, Owen ended up studying art in Paris, France, where he met Ruth. There is something about the meeting of a man and a woman from two different countries in a third country that is not their own who have a child together there that highlights the contingency and providence of human existence.

In The Seven Storey Mountain, Merton recounts how he was born into a mixed world. On the one hand, he was born into a veritable hell since the countryside was littered with the corpses of soldiers and the carcasses of horses and the Great

War, as it was known until World War II, raged on with no end in sight. At the same time, the countryside was the subject of some of Owen's best work. Thomas writes that his father painted like Paul Cézanne. It is likely that young Thomas acquired his sensitivity to the beauty of the natural world through his parents, through a combination of genes and careful instruction. Another way in which Merton was born into a mixed world is that he himself was mixed up. Merton describes himself in the following passage that is reminiscent of Augustine's Confessions: "Free by nature, in the image of God, I was nevertheless the prisoner of my own violence and my own selfishness" (The Seven Storey Mountain, 12).

Merton was baptized in Prades, France. Owen and Ruth had intended to live in France so that Owen could paint, but they did not stay there much longer; the war forced them to relocate. After he was barely a year old, they packed up and went to Bordeaux to get on a boat headed to New York. Initially staying with Ruth's parents, the Mertons eventually found their own place to stay. Since he was unable to support the family through his painting, Owen became what Thomas Merton calls a gardener, but what we would probably refer to as a landscaper today.

In 1918, the Mertons had their second child, John Paul Merton. Since he was too young, for Thomas to play with, Thomas decided to use his imagination to give himself company with an imaginary friend, Jack, and his imaginary dog, Doolittle. This disturbed his mother, however, when Thomas was afraid to cross the street because he was concerned that Doolittle would be struck by a real car.

By the age of five, young Thomas knew how to read, write, and draw. He especially liked to draw pictures of boats and sea-gulls. His favorite book was a volume called Greek Heroes, through which he was introduced to Theseus, Jason, Medusa, Perseus, and Andromeda. These stories sparked Thomas's imagination and his love of adventure.

Around this time, his grandmother came to visit them from New Zealand. She left a deep impression on Merton. In fact, it was his grandmother that taught him how to pray the "Our Father." At this time, the Mertons did not regularly attend church. His mother would often go to Quaker meetings on Sundays, but Thomas would remain home. Once, he asked his father if he could go to church, but the reply that he received was, "Some other Sunday." Thomas did make it to a Quaker meeting with his mother once, however. He was told that the people would be silent until the Holy Spirit moved one of them to speak, and that Dan Beard, one of the founders of the Boy Scouts of America, would be there. Thomas was more interested in seeing whether Dan Beard actually had a beard than how the Holy Spirit would move the people. To the delight of Thomas, Dan Beard actually had a beard.

Eventually, in 1921, Thomas made it to church somewhat regularly, but this was because his father took up a job as an organist at an Episcopal church. In addition to taking up this job, Owen also started to play the piano every evening in a movie theater. Thomas did not realize at the time that the reason why his father took up these jobs was because he had to pay for the doctor bills: Thomas's mother had stomach cancer.

The Death of Merton's Mother

There is perhaps no more significant event for a young person than the passing of one of his or her parents. This is certainly the case with Thomas. He was sheltered as much as possible from the reality that his mother was sick. He had not seen his mother in quite some time and did not exactly understand what was going on. It was his mother's idea that he not come to the hospital to visit her. His parents, or at least his mother, had a particular way of wanting to raise Thomas that included postponing his encounter with the reality of death for as long as reasonably possible.

The child was content to live at his grandparents' house; after all, there were woods to explore, dogs and cats to play with, woods to explore, and plenty of food to eat. In addition to this, with his father working and his mother in the hospital, Thomas took advantage of grandparent hospitality since, he remarks, he was "allowed to do more or less as I pleased" (Seven Storey Mountain, 24). He also confesses that he did not miss his mother very much. Most likely, a part of this was because of the novelty of the scenery and the pleasantness of the external circumstances in which he found himself.

At the same time, something was awry, even though Thomas did not know it until his father gave him a hand-written note from his mother. He had never received a note from his mother before, so the young boy was quite surprised. She explained to him that she was dying and that the two of them would never be able to see each other again. This was something that Thomas had to process on his own. He went out to the maple tree in the back of his grandparents' property and began to think about what all of this would mean for him. He remarks that he began to feel extremely depressed and that he could feel as though a big burden were placed on his shoulders. As for prayer, he says that the thought never even entered his mind and that it was only after an additional twenty years when he converted to Catholicism that he realized that he could and ought to pray for his mother.

His grandparents hired a car to bring them to the hospital so that they could see Ruth one last time. Thomas, however, was not allowed to go inside. Instead, he had to sit inside the car with the driver, the heavy rain pounding the roof of the car all the while. When his father and grandparents eventually returned, they were all dejected, and Thomas could deduce that his mother had in fact passed away. When they got home, Thomas followed his father and went to the door of the room he had entered; he saw his father weeping by the window.

Shortly after that, perhaps the following day, they went on another car trip. This time, Thomas was glad that he stayed in the car. His mother had requested to be cremated. In retrospect, he recalls how she had been impatient with useless things and how she had vigorously cleaned the house; this, Thomas speculates, is related to why she wanted to be cremated: she probably thought that the soulless body was useless and had to be done away with as quickly as possible. Regarding the actual funeral, Thomas mentions that it was raining and that although he was sad, he would have been far worse off had he seen his mother's coffin entering the furnace.

Although Ruth's death saddened Owen deeply, it truly opened up a new chapter of the Mertons' life, one that was less tied to mundane work and more aesthetic in its pretensions. Owen did not have to pay the doctor bills, which meant that he did not have to play the piano, play the organ, or work in gardens; instead, he could devote his time and energy to his first artistic love: painting. He was not restricted to a particular area, but could travel about as he pleased so that he could find new subjects to inspire his creativity. Life became quite nomadic for Owen and Thomas. They sailed frequently and moved constantly from one place to the next. Thomas loved it and thought that it was the most natural thing in the world, like the change of seasons or of the moon, to be moving around so often. He also had a lot of freedom at that time and enjoyed life immensely. It was in this varied and pleasant atmosphere that Thomas was raised during the next stage of his childhood.

Bermuda and New York

There was one time shortly after the death of Ruth when the Mertons lived for a while in Bermuda. Thomas attended a school there while Owen painted the landscapes. According to Michael W. Higgins, Bermuda was a "nightmare" for the Mertons; Higgins explains that Owen had an affair with Evelyn Scott, a novelist, who happened to be the wife of one of his friends and art associates, Cyril Kay Scott (Higgins, 5). Thomas found himself at odds with Evelyn Scott.

At his school in Bermuda, which happened to be a boarding school, Thomas was having a tremendously difficult time with his multiplication and division. In fact, because he could not wrap his mind around the concepts, his teacher would punish him frequently. Eventually, Owen pulled Thomas from the school in order to spend more time with him. Thomas was happy that he did not have to do his multiplication or division, but had to be vigilant so that his teacher would not see him and report him to the truant officer; whenever he saw her on her bicycle, he would jump into the bushes.

After this, Owen went to America for several months to sell his paintings, leaving Thomas in Bermuda with friends. When his father had finished selling his paintings at the exhibition in New York, he arranged for Thomas to come to New York.

There, he found out that his father's plan was to set sail for France with his friends and leave Thomas there in New York for some time.

Thomas recalls how he treated his brother, John Paul, during this time. Thomas was about nine years old, whereas John Paul was about five. Thomas had a group of friends, a gang as it were, who built a hut together. Naturally, John Paul wanted to join in and help his older brother. With remorse, Thomas writes that he and the other boys then threw stones in John Paul's direction. Their intention was not to hurt him; they merely wanted to convey the clear message that John Paul was not wanted. John Paul stood there at a distance, neither retreating nor advancing, looking at his brother with sad eyes.

Thomas's "gang" was not nearly large enough to challenge the established gang of Polish children in Little Neck. On one occasion, not all of Thomas friends were around and the Little Neck gang were near Thomas's clubhouse. In fact, they went all of the way up to Thomas's house, so Thomas and a few of his friends took refuge in the clubhouse. It was at this point, Thomas recalls, that John Paul walked from the front door of the Merton house, through the Little Neck gang with an air of dignity, and went straight to the clubhouse. Thomas and his friends did not turn him away; he was finally accepted.

Thomas was still not keen on religion. He relates that there were two prejudices present in his family regarding other religions, namely Judaism and Catholicism. He notes that his father's antipathy toward Catholicism was most likely influenced by his Masonic membership. Ironically, Owen's Masonic group was called the Knights Templars, who were originally a military religious order in the Catholic Church. Thomas says that he was negatively influenced by his father's anti-Catholicism and that even at a young age Thomas began to be suspicious of Catholicism.

During this time, Thomas's father was frequently abroad. He painted in various parts of Europe, as well as in Africa, while Thomas stayed in New York with his grandparents. One day, Thomas's grandfather told him he had received a letter informing him that Owen was seriously ill and on the verge of death. Thomas was old enough to understand the implications of this news and was understandably dejected. Owen recovered, however, and made it back to the United States.

He was, however, a different man. In fact, his renown as an artist was increasing more and more, and he was beginning to become somewhat of a celebrity in the art world. When Thomas saw Owen, the main thing he noticed was that he had a beard. "When are you going to shave it off?" Thomas asked him contemptuously? "I'm not!" his father replied. Owen eventually shaved it off several years later.

By this time, Thomas had become acclimatized to Douglaston and rather enjoyed being there. He had put down roots and was quite comfortable since he had numerous friends and enjoyed playing baseball (he had a Spalding bat), swimming, and taking pictures. He was also interested in joining the Boy Scouts. Thomas was therefore shocked when his father announced nonchalantly, "We are going to France." After vehemently protesting, Thomas sobbed. Owen comforted him by telling him that he would love France and that they were not going right away. Hoping that his father would ultimately change his mind, Thomas was consoled.

Nonetheless, they left for France on August 25, 1925, which happened to be the feast day of St. Louis of France, although Thomas was not aware of this significance when he left. France opened up a new chapter in Thomas's life.

France

When Owen and Thomas arrived in France, Thomas was not initially aware of the cultural richness of this country. Despite the lack of a deep impression, in his autobiography, Merton recalls the wealth of French culture:

> Even the countryside, even the landscape in France . . . seems to have been made full of a special perfection, as a setting for the best of the cathedrals, the most interesting of towns, the most fervent of monasteries, and the greatest of universities . . . [France] has possessed all the skills, from cooking to logic and theology, from bridge-building to contemplation, from vine-growing to sculpture, from cattle-breeding to prayer. (Seven Storey Mountain, 43)

Thomas soon fell in love with the cathedrals and the ruins of abbeys, even at his young age, and was impressed by the quaintness of the small town of Montauban even though his initial reaction was that it was a "dead town" (Seven Storey Mountain, 44).

The main reason why Owen decided to go to Montauban was because some friends of his recommended a school there called the Institut Jean Calvin. When Owen and Thomas visited it, however, Owen did not especially like it, and Thomas never ended up going there. Since Owen had been interested in settling in Montauban because of the school and because he wanted to paint—and he was not impressed with either the school or the surrounding landscape of the town itself—he decided to go somewhere else. Eventually, they settled in the ancient town of St. Antonin. What impressed Thomas about this town was that the church, which had an elegant and lofty spire stretching toward the heavens, was the centerpiece of the town.

Merton explains that one of the reasons why his father brought him to France was because he wanted to be a more involved father and did not want to leave his upbringing to others. In addition, Owen had something of a religious conversion, perhaps as the result of his near touch with death. He prayed more and asked Thomas to pray. In fact, Thomas found out later from some of Owen's friends that Owen was drawn to the Catholic Church at this time but decided not to convert because of what his family would think about it.

In 1926, Thomas's grandparents visited Owen and Thomas and brought John Paul along with them. They were interested in seeing France, Switzerland, and England, and invited Owen and Thomas to join them. Owen did not especially enjoy Switzerland. He found no landscapes that were in accordance with his artistic taste, and he did not have any time to paint even if he had wanted to. Typically, the first stops were at the museums, but Owen and Thomas also found them unsatisfactory. Thomas and John Paul eventually resorted to making fun of the items in the museums they visited. They were all quite happy when they returned to France from Switzerland.

When Thomas was eleven-and-a-half, he developed a crush on a local French girl named Henriette. She allowed him to chase him around a tree, and they enjoyed flirting with each other for some time. Shortly after this, however, his father heard about it and questioned Thomas about the affair. Just a few weeks later, Thomas was placed in a boarding school, the Lycée Ingres at Montauban. Immediately, the schoolchildren bullied the foreigner. Thomas writes that he learned a lot of French profanity simply from being the object of derision. Eventually, the children accepted him, but he was amazed by the sheer cruelty and brutality that many of the French children exhibited. He likens their fury to a kind of evil body of the devil that is analogous to the mystical body of Christ.

Thomas was able to find a group of friends who were more intellectual and precocious than the bullies in his school. They wrote novels (in French, naturally), and critiqued each other's plots. Thomas wrote one or two novels while he was at the boarding school in Montauban, although he did not share one of the plots with his friends since the villain of the novel was a Catholic priest in league with the Spanish Inquisition and he did not want to offend their Catholic sensibilities.

One winter, Thomas had a series of fevers. Being off on a painting expedition, Owen arranged for Thomas to stay with some of his friends, the Privats, who lived in Murat. The Privats were farmers. Simple, pious, and altogether good, they left a lasting impression on Thomas. They nursed him back to health by making sure that he had all of the fresh butter and milk that he needed and by attending to his needs. The Privats were so pious, good, and humble that Merton muses in his writings whether he owes his religious vocation to them.

One day in May of 1928, Owen got back from England and told Thomas to pack his bags since they were going to go to England. Thomas couldn't believe his good fortune! He gleefully told his companions at his school that he was going to be leaving soon, and they were all very happy for him, if not a little envious. While in the horse-drawn carriage, the clopping of the horses' hooves sounded like peels of liberty to the excited boy.

England

When they arrived in England, Thomas saw a billboard with an advertisement—written in English!—beckoning, "Visit Egypt!" He recounts nostalgically his love for England:

[T]he cockney cries of the porters and the smell of strong tea in the station refreshment room spelled out all the associations of what had, up to now, always been a holiday country for me, a land heavy with awe-inspiring proprieties, but laden with all kinds of comforts, and in which every impact of experience seemed to reach the soul through seven or eight layers of insulation. (Seven Storey Mountain, 79)

In addition to these comforts, Thomas enjoyed the convenience of finding himself in a world that communicated in his native tongue—not that languages posed any great difficulty to Thomas. Becoming an amateur novelist in a foreign language by the age of thirteen is an impressive intellectual feat. In addition to English and French, Merton eventually became fluent in Spanish, Portuguese, Italian, and Latin, and developed a reading knowledge of German and Greek.

One of Thomas's favorite persons at the time was his Aunt Maud, who lived in Ealing. He says that he "met very few people... so like an angel" (80). She was old and dressed conservatively, but he thought that she was an extremely kind person. He recalls a conversation that they had about his future: After she inquired about whether he had thought about his future, he replied that he was interested in becoming a writer, and more specifically a novelist. She replied that being a novelist can be a difficult business, but that perhaps he could find another job and write in his spare time, and that this was how many novelists got their start.

Although it was summer, the schools in England were still completing their summer term. Thomas was placed in a class in Ripley Court, where his classmates were quite suspicious of him since his father was an artist and he had been in school in France for the past two years. He had to suffer some humiliation on account of not knowing Latin in the slightest; he had to start at the most basic level in his study of the language. Yet, Thomas found that the English boys at Ripley were much pleasanter than the French children with whom he had gone to school in France. Since he needed to have enough Latin to get him through public school, Thomas had to stay in Ripley for two years.

Thomas recalls how he received some religion at this time. It was the first time he saw others saying prayers at their beds and the first time he had eaten meals after saying grace. He also heard one of his instructors read from Pilgrim's Progress on Sunday evenings. For the next two years, Thomas was a bit religious during a time when he direly needed spirituality.

After his stint at Ripley, Thomas went to a public school at Oakham, which was located in the English countryside. Owen was ill but had not received a diagnosis yet. Shortly after, Thomas received word that his father had a malignant brain tumor. His father asked Thomas to pray for him. Although in the years to come, doctors would develop practices that would allow them to take away portions of the brain safely, these techniques had not yet been discovered.

In Oakham, Thomas studied Cicero, Chaucer, and Shakespeare among other writers. F. C. Doherty, the new Headmaster at the school, encouraged Thomas to study for the Higher Certificate, which had no math on it. This was good for Thomas since he was not very good at math but excelled in languages. Doherty also encouraged Thomas to aim for a Cambridge scholarship. Thomas credits Doherty with preparing him the most for college.

One of the greatest influences on Thomas's thought was the poet William Blake. He was fascinated by Blake even though he could not quite understand him. He loved to read and think about Blake's poetry, which in hindsight he described as more profound than he had at first realized. For Thomas, Blake was a channel of grace through which God worked in a mysterious way, despite his heterodoxies. In his words, "The Providence of God was eventually to use Blake to awaken something of faith and love in my own soul" (Seven Storey Mountain, 110).

In 1930, Thomas's family members had a serious discussion about the family business and included Thomas in the discussion. Their finances, like everyone's finances, were adversely affected by the Great Depression. Owen made sure that Thomas and John Paul would be provided for and showed Thomas the figure that he would inherit. Amazed at his father's generosity, Thomas accepted this with graciousness, but ended up squandering much of it.

When the holidays came around, Thomas stayed with Tom, his godfather. The schedule in Tom and his wife's apartment in London consisted of being served breakfast in bed by a French maid at about nine in the morning, taking a bath afterward, and searching for entertainment later on. Thomas enjoyed going to the museum or the park. After this, they would reconvene for lunch at the apartment.

At one point in the summer, they visited Owen in the hospital. Thomas asked him how he was, but Owen merely looked at him with a confused expression and did not answer. It was evident that Owen could no longer speak. Seeing him so helpless crushed Thomas's spirit, and he wept for his father. Owen likewise wept. For the rest of the summer, they religiously visited Owen once or twice a week. Once, Thomas found Byzantine drawings, sketched icons, that his father had made. He muses in his autobiography that his father was communing with God in a way that he had never done before.

Shortly after, when Thomas had started up school again, he received a telegram informing him that his father had died. His godfather had an obituary printed in the papers and prepared the funeral for Owen. Like his mother, Thomas's father was also cremated. Thomas was not exactly sure how to interpret these events. It turns out that he subconsciously saw himself as completely free once his father died, but he writes that it would take several more years before he was able to recognize what kind of spiritual slavery he was in.

America, Germany, and a Close Call

The inheritance Owen left to Thomas enabled him to travel extensively. He made use of his money to travel periodically to the United States. He also went to Germany and Italy. His experiences abroad influenced him tremendously. His soul was hungry for experiences, beauty, and the zest of life, and his encounters with different cultures broadened his cultural awareness and connected him to his familial, societal, and religious roots. One trip, as we shall see, left a profound spiritual impact on him, and that was his trip to Italy. Before recounting this trip, however, we will first look at one of his voyages to the United States, a vacation he took in Germany, and a brush with death he experienced in England after his return from Germany.

On his way to visit his grandparents in the United States, Thomas, who was now sixteen years old, became infatuated with a young woman from California. He thought that she was about his age since she seemed so young, but as it turns out, she was almost twice his age. She was content to socialize with him, however; she even attempted to teach him bridge. For his part, he told her and her friends about his ambitions. Toward the end of the trip, he professed his love for her, and she replied that he simply did not know what he was saying and that they would never see each other again after the voyage. He interpreted this as \ meaning that he should not be so inane and should keep a tighter rein on himself before he did something truly foolish. Crushed, Thomas went back to his cabin and cried. He even tried to get a photograph of the woman, but to his consternation the image turned out blurry. When his family picked him up, he was reticent and depressed, which caused a chasm to develop between them. He spent most of his time away from his family and frequented the streets. He even went to some burlesque shows in the evening, which indicates something of the state his soul was in. When he came back to England, he was full of pride, thinking that he knew more than not only his classmates, but also his teachers.

During Easter vacation in 1932, Thomas went to Germany. He was studying Spinoza during this trip. He visited Cologne and journeyed to Koblenz on foot. It was during this trip that he developed some pain in one of his toes, but he ignored it. According to Higgins, it was during this trip that Thomas encountered some Nazis. Higgins elaborates:

> He was meandering . . . near Koblenz when a car came
> speedily upon him crammed full of several youths
> clenching their fists and hollering at him. They were

Hitler Youth and very likely future officers of the SS and they were inviting him in their thuggish way to vote for Hitler as the next German Chancellor. As quickly as they descended upon him, they disappeared. (10)

This encounter left an impression on Thomas of the nefariousness of the Nazis.

When he returned to England, Thomas had an illness, which he initially thought was the result of a toothache and a sore foot. He was sent to the dentist who ended up taking out his tooth without anesthesia. Instead of getting better, the wound in his mouth developed into gangrene. The doctor came and did what he could to excise it. Thomas lay in bed that night, thinking that death was right next to him, but he approached this frightening scenario with apathy. Eventually, Thomas recovered, which he writes was a great blessing since he was fortunate not to have perished at this time in his life when his soul was full of sins. What kind of sins did he engage in? He read smutty novels, liked to drink in excess, was selfish, and was full of pride. Fortunately for Thomas, he was restored to health. Although he did not see the religious significance of this episode at the time, later on he recognized that it was only by the grace of God that he survived so that he could have a chance to enter the Catholic Church and convert from his immoral ways.

In June, Thomas took his test for the Higher Certificate, which tested his knowledge of French, German, and Latin. In fact, the test was given in these languages. He had enough knowledge of these languages to pass with no problem. In December, Thomas took a scholarship exam at Cambridge. He passed this exam as well and won a scholarship to Cambridge. His future was paved: he was to attend Clare College at Cambridge and to make something of himself. As we shall see in the next chapter, however, this was not to be the case.

Freed from Oakham, Thomas celebrated by gorging himself on food and drink to such an extent that he made himself sick. This episode of overindulging was actually a better indication than his successful exams of what was to come in Cambridge. On his eighteenth birthday, in 1933, Tom took him to a café, and the following day he departed for Italy.

Italy

Italy was, for Thomas, a chance to fill his soul with the history and culture of lost worlds; his purpose was essentially secular since he had no interest in the churches of Rome at the time. Despite this secular beginning, however, Thomas's journey somehow evolved into a kind of pilgrimage, since during this trip he had the first deep religious experience in his life.

Young and extravagant, Thomas spent a lot of money and was not very careful with it; frugality was not one of the young man's virtues. In fact, at one point he likens himself to the prodigal son in the Gospels. While at Avignon, Thomas wrote to Tom asking for money since he knew that he was going to run out soon. When Thomas got the money, he also got a letter from Tom rebuking him for being so reckless with the money. Merton recounts that while he was a teenager, he "believed in the beautiful myth about having a good time so long as it does not hurt anybody else" (Seven Storey Mountain, 129). It took him years to understand that this is blatantly false. This was also the first indication of a rift between Thomas and Tom.

After Thomas received the money, he journeyed to Rome by way of Genoa and Florence. Once he arrived, he attempted to reconstruct in his mind how ancient Rome looked. This was a difficult task because of all of the shouting from the postcard vendors. He concluded that ancient Rome was an extremely ugly city. After this he read through a learned book on Rome, wandered about its museums, and read his novels in the evenings. After about a week, Thomas decided to look at the churches instead of the ruins. This opened him up to a much different ancient Rome than he had earlier envisioned.

Exploring the frescoes in one of the chapels near the base of the Palatine awoke Thomas's fascination with the ancient churches. He was especially moved by an impressive mosaic overhead of Christ coming on the clouds of heaven to judge the living and the dead. The Byzantine mosaics captured Thomas's imagination and his aesthetic sensitivity. Not having had much religious instruction himself, Merton writes that he still learned something of religion simply by gazing on the frescoes and mosaics, reflecting that this makes sense because they were designed to instruct the illiterate. It was at this time that Thomas began to have some sort of intimation of who Christ really is. In fact, he was so moved that he bought a copy of the Vulgate, the official Latin version of the Bible, and began reading it instead of his other books. He began reading the Gospels and started visiting the churches not simply for their architectural beauty but for the peace they afforded his soul. Still, he had not yet experienced anything like a conversion.

One evening while Thomas was in his room in Rome, it seemed to him that his father was somehow present in the room. It dawned upon him that his soul was in a seriously depraved state and that he needed to change his ways. He began to pray and ask God to save him from the slavery he was in. It was for him, he writes, a great grace from God, but that he unfortunately did not persevere. Although he had not prayed in any of the churches that he visited in Rome, he began to pray in them the next day. After walking out of one of the churches, he felt as though he had been reborn. Shortly after this he visited a Trappist monastery outside of Rome. It was at this point that he first thought he would like to be a Trappist monk. When he related this thought to the mother of one of his friends on the bus ride back, she gave him a look of horror. As destiny would have it, Thomas did end up becoming a Trappist monk, but this would not be for several more years.

When he returned to England, Thomas covertly read the Bible since he wanted neither to be made fun of nor to receive any approval. He still sought God in his own way by visiting a Quaker house. Thomas's religious experience in Rome was key to his formal conversion, and it was a great grace that prepared him for his life to come.

Soon, however, his religious fervor grew tepid and he fell back to some of his old ways. When he went to America, he confesses that he would hang out at the burlesque. He also spent time with Reginald Marsh and attended many parties in New York. When the summer was over, he made his way back to England to attend Cambridge.

Cambridge

Looking back on Cambridge, Merton describes it in tones of disgust. There was a "stench of corruption" at Cambridge, but Thomas's "blind appetites" led him to "rush in and take a huge bite of this rotten fruit," the awful taste of which lingered with him for years (Seven Storey Mountain, 147).

Thomas's experience at Cambridge was, from a secular point of view, a disaster. Not taking his studies seriously, he was intent on experiencing all that an eighteen-year-old boy could want. Instead of studying for his language tests, which he ended up passing anyway, he would read Freud and Jung while inebriated. He determined that the reason why he was an introvert and was unhappy was because he experienced sexual repression, from which he attempted to liberate himself.

Merton does not elaborate on his sexual escapades in The Seven Storey Mountain, but as it turns out, a rumor began that he fathered an illegitimate child while he was at Cambridge. Another rumor in Columbia University, the second institution of higher education that he attended, claimed that he had fathered two illegitimate children. The likely truth of the matter is that he did father an illegitimate child, but not more than one. This has happened before in the history of converts;

perhaps the most famous example is St. Augustine of Hippo, who fathered an illegitimate child, Adeodatus, whom Augustine ended up burying when the child died as a teenager.

From a religious point of view, Merton's experience at Cambridge was simultaneously disastrous and essential to his religious conversion. It was disastrous since he found himself wallowing in moral squalor; but it was transformative since he found himself at the bottom of the barrel. The bitterness of his experience served as a catalyst that ultimately led to his conversion.

Apart from wasting his time and skipping lectures, he was morally lost. The one good thing that he acquired from Cambridge, he writes, was his acquaintance with Dante's Inferno and Purgatorio. He read them closely with fascination, but his soul was in such a state that although he could entertain the premises of the stories easily enough, they had no impact on his soul.

During his year in Cambridge, Thomas's Aunt Maud died, which signified to him the death of his childhood. She had long been there to listen to him and to lead him through the pleasantries of the English countryside, but without her, England itself seemed dead. To Merton, not only was Cambridge rotten, but the whole system in England was rotten to the core. In shockingly strong terms, he describes what is, in his opinion, the matter with England. "What was wrong with this place, with all these people?" asks Merton, "Why was everything so empty" (Seven Storey Mountain, 156)? Merton answers his own question as follows:

> Cambridge and, to some extent, the whole of England was pretending . . . to act as if it were alive. And it took a lot of acting. It was a vast and complicated charade . . . the people were morally dead, asphyxiated by the steam of their own strong yellow tea, or by the smell of their own pubs or breweries, or by the fungus on the walls of Oxford and Cambridge. (Seven Storey Mountain, 156)

Shortly after this scathing critique of the spirit of England, however, Merton tempers it by adding that perhaps World War II did something to revive England's moral deficiencies and made it a better place. What is Merton's proof that it was a rotten place?

He had a friend, Mike, who was athletic, loved to eat and drink, and passionately chased after the young women. His trademark was that he liked to punch his fist through windows. When Thomas had been gone from Cambridge for about a year, he heard that someone found Mike dangling in the showers of one of the buildings from a piece of rope that he had placed over the pipes and wrapped around his neck: Mike had committed suicide. Such was the turpitude and vacuity that characterized Cambridge in Merton's mind.

Toward the end of the academic year, Thomas received letters from Tom, his guardian. Each letter was sharper than the one before. Finally, Tom summoned Thomas to come down to meet him in London. He went to the waiting room (Tom was a doctor) and waited to be summoned. After nearly an hour and a half, he was finally called and went upstairs to see Tom. When he walked in, Tom offered him a cigarette, as though to suggest that he was going to need it. Being a defiant teenager, Thomas declined. For the next twenty minutes, which Merton describes as the "most painful and distressing [time] I have ever lived through"(Seven Storey Mountain, 154), Thomas was forced to explain his conduct, though he merely stammered and gave lame excuses. Once he was out of Tom's office and out on the streets, he smoked quite a few cigarettes.

After the school year, Thomas went to America. He had planned on going back to Cambridge the next year, but received a letter from Tom advising that he not come back to Cambridge since it would be a waste of time and money; instead, he recommended that Thomas stay in America. Thomas agreed and ultimately decided to enroll in Columbia University.

Columbia I

Merton was still in the midst of his conversion. It is not as though a bolt of thunder came crashing down and he was suddenly converted; instead, the process was a rather long and arduous one. The odd thing about his conversion is that in the middle of it, he became a Communist.

For Merton, the solution to his moral deficiencies was to adopt Communism. This was an easy solution for him since it essentially allowed him to blame society rather than himself for his faults. It was the materialistic society in which he lived that had produced him, or so he thought. He writes that although he recognizes that society shares some of the responsibility, the underlying vices that he had, such as lust and greed, are realities that are present to every society, regardless of its moral fiber or lack thereof. Merton fell for communism because he could not distinguish the veracity of the evils that Communism tried to remedy from the incorrectness of its diagnosis and prescription for the ailments plaguing society. In short, he started hanging out with the Communist crowd.

In comparison to Cambridge, Columbia was a breath of fresh air for Merton. Whereas at Cambridge there was an emphasis on fancy academic regalia, at Columbia this showiness was stripped down and reduced to special occasions. The students at Columbia were apparently more genuine, more appreciative of the education they were receiving, and more industrious than their Cambridge counterparts.

The person who most influenced Merton at Columbia was Mark Van Doren, a literature professor who had a scholastic bent, being familiar with Jacques Maritain and Etienne Gilson and being friends with Richard McKeon and Mortimer Adler. Van Doren's quasi-scholasticism, which led him to search for the essence of things, prevented him from being swept away by subjective interpretations of literary works. Merton writes that luckily for him, he encountered Van Doren; had he not met the professor, he would have been too docile and would have been swept away completely by his new adherence to Communism.

Although Merton disagrees with the legend that Columbia University was a stronghold for Communism at the time, he does mention that they had some sway at the university and that the school newspaper was controlled by Communists. Merton's brief association with Communism consisted of picketing, engaging in a so-called Peace Strike, and making a speech at one of the Communist meetings, as well as joining the Young Communist League. A girl encouraged him to follow her to the liquor store, after which she signed him up for this group. He went to just one meeting of the Young Communist League; the subject of the meeting was so inane that he walked out, got a beer, and enjoyed a cigarette. This was the extent of Merton's career as a revolutionary.

Merton participated in several extra-curricular activities while he was at Columbia, more notably as a writer for several school newspapers, and less notably in cross country. Merton worked for The Spectator, The Review, and Jestor, the school newspapers at Columbia. Merton joined the cross-country team but was never much good at it. He finished nearly last in every race. In fact, he would come across the finish line when most of the spectators had already left. Perhaps the reason for this was how he spent his nights: he joined a fraternity and began hanging out in bars that played jazz several times a week. The appeal was the sensory overload—the sea of bodies, the throbbing music, the effects of alcohol, and the liveliness of the atmosphere. There was not much talking, perhaps because of the loudness of the music, and the people simply sat together drinking. The fluidity of this medium of people can be sensed in some of Reginald Marsh's paintings.

As far as his spiritual life was concerned, Merton describes himself as not doing very well. He maintained the same vices, but was still searching in his own way for God. Still full of himself, he filled the yearbook with pictures of himself and was proud of the fact that everyone at Columbia knew who he was. In looking back, he would be amazed that people did not mock him for his vanity. One of his most humiliating experiences was when a girl he was in love with drove off with another group of men shortly after telling him that she did not want to go out.

Merton was poised more than ever for a religious conversion, even if he did not know that he especially needed one or of where he ought to look. Perhaps the main event that led to his conversion is that he happened upon a book that would leave a profound impact on him—namely, Etienne Gilson's The Spirit of Medieval Philosophy.

Columbia II

At this point in his life, Merton still had some strong biases toward the Catholic Church. Although it is true that he had experienced something like a conversion during his vacation in Rome, he was more inspired about what Christianity was and stood for, as well as the message of the Gospels, than he was enamored of what Catholicism was; these are two different things. One of Merton's biases was against the imprimatur, i.e. the permission of a bishop to have a book printed because it is in line with the doctrine of the Catholic Church.

One day, Merton was walking by a Scribner's bookstore when was drawn in by the beauty of the new books. One of the books he bought was The Spirit of Medieval Philosophy. When he was on the train, he opened the book and, as it turned out, there was an imprimatur on the first page. He admits that he would never have bought the book had it been advertised as Catholic; however, he ended up reading the book. Although he felt deceived, he recognized the hand of providence in this since the book opened up a different perspective on Catholicism for Merton.

The central idea that Merton took from Gilson's book was the medieval concept of aseity, i.e. the ability of some entity to exist in virtue of itself without dependence on any other being. This quality was understood by the scholastics to be only applicable to God. In other words, God is pure being itself.

One of the effects this had on Merton was to disillusion him about his notion that Catholic belief was superstitious nonsense; he now realized that Catholicism is philosophically grounded and intellectually tenable. The stock of Catholicism suddenly soared in Merton's estimation. When he had finished reading through the book, he decided that he needed to pray to seek God. Instead of going to a Catholic Church, however, he went to an Episcopal Church, Zion Church, where his father had played the organ when he was a boy. He did not attend frequently however, and was not impressed with the minister, who seemed to want to dilute Christian doctrines such as the Trinity and the Incarnation.

Back at Columbia in the fall of 1936, Merton stepped into a classroom that was not the right class—it was Van Doren's Shakespeare course instead. As he got up to leave, something beckoned him to him to stay for the duration of the class, and when he was done, he registered for the course. Merton says that it was best college course he had ever taken. The students in the course dove into themes such as love and hatred, life and death, time and eternity, and all of the other topics that Shakespeare touches on in his plays. During this same academic year, Merton made several friends who did him a lot of good: Robert Lax, Ed Rice, Seymour Freedgood, Bob Gibney, and Bob Gerdy. All of them were friends with Mark Van Doren, although Van Doren was not the nexus that united them; rather, each of them in their own way was searching for God.

An important book that influenced Merton greatly was Aldous Huxley's Ends and Means. Huxley's conclusion, namely that in order for human beings to avoid living like wild animals they must pray and practice asceticism, was revolutionary for Merton. He had thought that asceticism was a kind of masochism performed by people who did not enjoy life. What Huxley did for Merton was to show that asceticism was more about detachment than it was about physical mortifications, and that this detachment is central to changing the world and maintaining equilibrium in human society. It was also Huxley's book that influenced Merton to look toward the East for spiritual wisdom since Huxley often referred to Buddhist traditions. Merton, as a result, got his hands on all of the books on Eastern mysticism that he could find.

Steeping himself in Oriental mysticism, Merton was pleased to find that at Cambridge a Hindu monk by the name of Doctor Bramachari. He had been sent to the World Congress of Religions in Chicago and ended up acquiring a Ph.D. in Vaishnava Theology from the University of Chicago five years later. Merton was impressed with him, and they built a rapport together. Bramachari explained to Merton that the reason why Christian missionaries were not successful in India is because they did not live poor, simple lives and most of them ate meat, something that is reprehensible to Hindus. In light of the success of the work of Mother Teresa of Calcutta, Bramachari's assessment seems to have been right on target. Bramachari knew that Merton was searching for God and encouraged him to read St. Augustine's Confessions and The Imitation of Christ.

Merton eventually checked out The Imitation of Christ in a library and added it to his reading list. All the while, he was working on his thesis on William Blake and was also reading Jacques Maritain. His thought was becoming more and more engrossed in scholasticism, and he was drawn more and more to the Catholic Church. One day, Merton decided to go to Mass for the first time in his life. He stepped into the church and knelt down without genuflecting. The Mass was in Latin, since it was before Vatican II, and the priest gave a sermon on the divinity of Christ, something that had resonated with Merton ever since the time he had seen the mosaics on the apses of the churches in Rome. When it came time for the consecration of the Eucharistic species and the bells started to chime, Merton rushed out, afraid that he was not supposed to be present during the Mysteries. He did not go back to church for some time, but ultimately was drawn to seek a priest. He found one, Father Ford, and told him that he wanted to become Catholic.

Conversion to Catholicism

So it was that Merton began his journey toward becoming a Catholic. He attended catechism classes two evenings a week and progressed through the study of the faith. His teacher was Fr. Moore, the priest who had said the first mass he attended. Merton indicates that he had thought about becoming a priest during his conversion process, but did not dare mention this thought to Fr. Ford or Fr. Moore; instead, he confided in a layman, Daniel Walsh, who was a professor of philosophy, but only quite a bit later on.

Merton took a course on St. Thomas Aquinas that Walsh taught. A Thomist, Walsh had the privilege of knowing and collaborating with Etienne Gilson and Jacques Maritain. Walsh called Merton an Augustinian, meaning that his bent was not toward the intellectual and speculative but toward the spiritual and practical. Merton writes that Walsh had the rare quality of being able to appreciate all of the different schools of Catholic philosophy and theology without insisting that a particular school is better than all of the others.

Merton was baptized on November 16, 1938. Ed Rice was his godfather, and Lax, Seymour, and Gerdy, who were Jews, joined Merton after the ceremony. The ceremony itself was deep and pregnant with meaning. The priest blew on him and exorcised him. Commenting on this experience, Merton writes that more than seven demons must have flown out from him at that time.

Although he was a Catholic, Merton writes that he essentially lived the same life after his baptism as before. He received the sacraments, but did not enter into the depths of prayer as he should have. Essentially, although he had undergone an intellectual conversion, his will still had to be converted. Moreover, Merton lacked a solid devotion to Our Lady during the first year of his conversion. Although he believed in the doctrines that the Church taught regarding her, he did not realize how powerful her intercession was and how central of a role she had in God's plan of salvation since all graces pass through her because she is the Mother of God, who is the source of all goodness.

Merton's deeper conversion began when he had a conversation with Robert Lax about the purpose of writing. Merton wanted to be known for his writing; basically, he was interested in fame. Lax, on the other hand, had an entirely different reason for writing: for Lax, writing was for the sake of bettering society. Human beings, in his view, need to be told of God in a clear way that did not seem superstitious but that made sense to them and was backed by authority. Lax asked Merton what he wanted, and when he said to be a good Catholic, Lax replied that what he should want is to be a saint. When Merton replied that he thought this was too radical and did not know how to do this, Lax said that the only thing he had to do to be a saint is to want it. Merton was dumbfounded, but it impressed him deeply. Still, he tucked away this principle in the shelves of his mind and did not immediately change.

At that time, Merton was living by what he called a two-column principle, i.e. a way of looking at the world that divides actions into mortal sins and venial sins. Since there are some sins that are not mortal, such as drinking alcohol to an extent that is not quite drunkenness, the logic behind this principle is that if it is not a mortal sin, then it is permitted, and that if someone says that it is not permitted, then this statement is heretical.

In 1939, Merton saw Bramachari set sail with the cardinals who were travelling to elect a new pope (the new pope the cardinals elected was Pope Pius XII). He got a studio apartment and began to work on his Ph.D. He planned to write a dissertation on Gerard Manley Hopkins. In the summer,

Merton and his friends stayed at a cottage and borrowed books from the library of Fr. Irenaeus, a Franciscan priest at St. Bonaventure's College. There they set up their typewriters, wrote during the day, and entertained themselves in the evening. This was how they spent their summer.

When they returned and went back to Columbia, things were different: News was buzzing about a possible war. In September, Merton received news that Warsaw had been bombed and that World War II was officially underway. At the time, he felt as though he was partially to blame for the war on account of his sins, so he went to confession and Mass.

During this time, Merton was starting to think about the priesthood. He had the idea that he was going to be a priest, although when he casually mentioned it, Gibney thought that that he was just making a joke. One day he went to the church of St. Francis Xavier and went into a lower church where there was Eucharistic adoration. The Blessed Sacrament was exposed, and the people were singing Tantum Ergo, the hymn composed by St. Thomas Aquinas. Merton joined them, and he suddenly became aware that he had a momentous decision to make. Merton looked at the Host and told God that he wanted to be a priest and asked him to make him one if it was his will. This signified a profound transition point in Merton's life.

Which Religious Order?

Merton confided in Dan Walsh about his desire to be a priest. Walsh was pleased and said that he had always thought Merton had a vocation to the priesthood. They began discussing different religious orders, and Merton did his own research, looking at the Catholic Encyclopedia entries on the Dominicans, Franciscans, Jesuits, and Benedictines. He did not think that the Jesuits were for him because they were too active and military for his tastes; Merton had a spirit that needed to explore, expand, grow, and experience an extent of freedom and independence that the Jesuit order would not have permitted. Merton needed solitude. While he was attracted to the Benedictines, he was worried that they possibly might not be the best for him because he could end up being separated from the communal liturgical life and be stuck as a parish priest.

Walsh then brought up the Franciscans. Merton thought that they would be a good fit for him since they lived simple and informal lives. He also liked their Rule since it was easy, and was drawn to the lyricism of their spirit. Furthermore, his association with St. Bonaventure's had given him some insight into their way of life.

Their conversation then turned to the Order of Cistercians, or as they are sometimes called, the Trappists. This was the order that elicited the most respect from Walsh. In fact, he had gone on a retreat at a Trappist monastery in Kentucky called Our Lady of Gethsemani. When Walsh brought up the idea to Merton, Merton was perplexed. He did not like the idea of fasting so much and thought that all of the silence would be unhealthy. Walsh explained that they sang the Liturgy of the Hours several times a day in choir and that the monks made their own food. Although they were essentially vegetarians, only eating meat when they got sick, they were very healthy. Merton recoiled from this idea. The irony is that not only was Merton to become a Trappist, but he was also to join the very monastery where Walsh had been on retreat.

At the end of their conversation, Merton and Walsh were agreed that Merton should approach the Franciscans. Walsh gave him the phone number of Fr. Edmund, a Franciscan friend of his, who was at the monastery of St. Francis of Assisi. Merton met Fr. Edmund and had some conversations with him. He was eager to enter the novitiate, but was told that he would have to wait until the next November since all of the novitiates entered at the same time. Although he was disappointed, he continued his Ph.D. work and started attending daily Mass. He was starting to become happier in his life even though the change was almost imperceptible to him. It took one of his friends to point out that he looked very happy. He also started to do the Stations of the Cross. Furthermore, he did The Spiritual Exercises of St. Ignatius of Loyola by himself in his room. His interior life was starting to blossom, and he found opportunities everywhere to pray to God, whether it was going to Mass, praying the Rosary, doing the Stations of the Cross, or doing spiritual reading. In addition to his prayers and studies, Merton taught a class in English composition at Columbia University. And so he passed the time, eagerly awaiting the day when he would be able to enter the Franciscan novitiate.

As the time was drawing closer for him to enter the novitiate, Merton was allowed to access the Franciscans' philosophy room, where he would study St. Thomas Aquinas's Summa Theologica and where there was a crucifix that his eyes could see once he lifted them from the text. These were some of the happiest days that Merton had ever experienced. And yet, something was not quite right. The reason why he had wanted to become a Franciscan was because he thought that the life was easy, that he would be able to keep the Rule and have access to natural comforts. In other words, he was not laying down his life, picking up the cross, and following Jesus; there was no sacrifice involved. Furthermore, Merton began to realize that Dan Walsh and Fr. Edmund did not really know what he had been through and what type of person he had been. To top things off, after experiencing about six months of spiritual consolation, all at once, he was dry. When he met Fr. Edmund again to discuss his vocation and bring up his doubts, Fr. Edmund told him to let him think and pray over what he had told him and to come back the next day. When Merton came back, Fr. Edmund told him that he should write the Provincial to inform him that he was reconsidering his vocation.

Devastated and confused, Merton found a Capuchin church, went inside, and went to confession. He tried to explain to the priest what he was going through, but the priest got the story mixed up and thought that Merton had done something awful and that he was being kicked out of religious life. Also, Merton gave him the impression that he was merely complaining and that he was therefore making a mockery of the sacrament of reconciliation. As a result, the perturbed priest told him that he surely had no vocation to be a religious or a priest. Merton wept as he walked outside the confessional and prayed in front of the tabernacle. Although Merton experienced quite a bit of turmoil in his soul at the time, he later recognized that it was not God's will for him to be a Franciscan.

Back to the Drawing Board

Although he was crushed and thought that he did not have a vocation to be a priest or, apparently, a religious, Merton was intent on living a life of grace and contemplation as a lay person. He thought about joining a Third Order and purchased a set of breviaries. His goal was to teach at a Catholic school, live under the same roof as the Blessed Sacrament, and say the Liturgy of the Hours every day. With this intention, he acquired a job at St. Bonaventure's and taught a literature class to football players and seminarians.

The students were genuine Catholics but Merton was often surprised at their opinions. For instance, one did not believe that humility was a virtue and most of them believed that their civilization was the best one in the history of the human race. Overall, however, the students were good young people, and Merton was sorry to see the war affect them.

Merton's brother thought that he would receive a commission by joining the Navy, but it did not come so easily. John Paul and the Navy had a falling out, and John Paul was happy to be back in the United States after sailing to the West Indies. After this, he decided to go to Mexico to photograph the Mayan temples.

Meanwhile, Thomas had the idea that he would go on retreat during Holy Week and Easter. After considering this prospect for a while, he decided that there was only one place he wanted to go on retreat: the Trappist monastery in Kentucky that Dan Walsh had talked about. After he inquired, Merton received a reply from the Trappists that he was welcome to come for a retreat. Almost at the same time, he received something else in the mail: a letter from the draft board. He filled out the papers and informed the army that he would be happy to assist them as a non-combatant, which the law permitted; he even quoted St. Thomas Aquinas to justify his stance. Merton had come a long way from where he was during his years as a nominal Communist to this point, where he was willing to aid the United States war effort against the Nazis and their then-allies, the Soviet Communists. As it turned out, when Merton was examined by the army doctors, they informed him that the army did not want him because he did not have enough teeth!

When the time came nearer for Merton to make his retreat at the Trappist monastery, he looked up the Trappists in the Catholic Encyclopedia. When he read about the Trappists, Cistercians, Carthusians, and Camaldolese, his heart was set ablaze. He was astounded that there were men who still sought solitude in the world and who strove to live pure lives by giving up everything. The thought of these holy men pierced Merton's heart like a sword since he knew, or at least he thought he knew, that he did not have a vocation. And yet, the desire was there.

When it came time for him to go on retreat with the Trappists, Merton first went to Cincinnati and from there took a train to Louisville. When he got to the monastery grounds, a monk asked him if he was staying permanently, to which Merton replied that he wasn't. When he stepped into the monastery, he felt as though he were entering another world, or more precisely, as though he were leaving the realm of the world. The silence was as tangible as it was profound. What impressed Merton the most was the solemnity of the liturgical celebrations. His heart was so full of joy that he thought it might explode. As the retreat ended, he prayed the Stations of the Cross and at the fourteenth station, he prayed that if it were God's will, that he would be allowed to become a Trappist.

When he went out of the monastery and was back at Louisville, he felt as though he had descended a high mountain peak: the world was much different than where he had come from. He saw the people hustling and bustling about, and had an innate sense of the futility of their restlessness. Back at St. Bonaventure's, a thought came to him that he should consult the Scriptures to ask what God wanted of him. He picked up the Bible, said a brief prayer, opened the Bible, closed his eyes, and pointed on one of the pages. The words that he saw were: "Ecce eris tacens," which means, "Behold, you will be silent." The angel had just announced to Zechariah that he would be struck dumb because he did not believe in God. Merton saw this message as somewhat ambiguous. On the one hand, it seemed a clear sign that he should enter the Trappist monastery since he associated the Trappists with silence (also, he noted a resemblance between the words 'Trappist' and 'tacens'). On the other hand, Zechariah was receiving a reproof and Merton wondered whether God was reproving him as well.

Meanwhile, John Paul had made his way back from Mexico. He had gone to the Yucatan and Puebla, and had come back with Mexican records, souvenirs, pictures, and a revolver with which he shot a poisonous snake that was six feet away from him. Thomas learned that his brother was thinking about becoming a Catholic, but he seemed indecisive about it. After their brief meeting, John Paul drove back to Ithaca to prepare for his next school year at Cornell.

Harlem and Gethsemani

One day at St. Bonaventure's, Merton noticed that a crowd had gathered around a woman who was giving a speech. At first he thought it was odd. Nuns, priests, and students were gathered around her, and they were completely mesmerized by her words. As he drew closer, he began to hear her message and he knew that she had to be the Baroness. Catherine de Hueck, or Catherine Doherty as she had come to be known through her second marriage (her first marriage had been annulled since she had originally married her first cousin), was born in Russia and was actually a baroness. A Byzantine Catholic, she fled Communist Russia and sought refuge in the United States. At the time when she gave that speech, she had started Friendship House in Harlem, which was dedicated to fostering interracial understanding and sharing the love of Christ.

The theme of the Baroness's speech that Merton heard was that if Catholics lived their faith as they should and saw things with spiritual eyes, they would not be able to stay away from Harlem because that was where poverty, misery, and injustice were affecting one particular race; that was where Catholics could find the face of Christ. Since Catholics were not especially concerned with Harlem, however, Communists had entrenched themselves there and transformed it into a bastion for their cause. The Communists persuaded the

African Americans that it was actually the Communists, not the Catholic Church, who cared for the poor. In fact, the Communists even used the social encyclicals of the popes to convince their hearers that the Catholics were not on the side of the poor because Catholics did not evidently follow the teachings of these encyclicals.

Merton was very impressed by the Baroness. He got a sense that the Holy Spirit was living in her and inspiring her every action. At the end of the speech, Merton approached her and asked her if it would be all right if he were to go to Friendship House sometime. She said that it would be fine, and he started to go in the evenings. His task was essentially to look after the children. He played piano, drew pictures for the kids, and told them stories.

After going on a retreat at a Trappist monastery in Canada, Merton went with some priests to pick up the Baroness from a train station in Canada and bring her back to New York. When they were all together in the car, she turned to Merton and asked him when he was going to relocate permanently to Harlem. The question took him by surprise, but he eventually began to be convinced that this was what he should do. As a result, he resigned from his post at St. Bonaventure's.

Even before going to Harlem, however, Merton gained the insight that he in fact had a vocation—since every time he was asked if he was going to be a priest, he experienced pain at what he thought was the fact that he didn't have a vocation. He knew that he wanted to be a Trappist. Shortly after going to Harlem, Merton was set to go on a retreat at the Trappist monastery of Gethsemani in Kentucky for Advent, but his purpose in going was actually to enter the monastery. He informed the Baroness of his decision in a letter dated December 6, 1941. He closed his accounts, burned some of his manuscripts, gave other manuscripts away, and headed to Kentucky. When he was there, the monk who had greeted him at the beginning of his first retreat recognized him and asked him whether he was going to stay for good this time, to which Merton replied that he would so long as the brothers would pray for him. Merton entered the monastery, was interviewed by the novice master, and eventually acquired the Trappist habit and began his life as a monk, taking the religious name "Louis."

He was very happy with his new life of work and contemplation, but what made it sweeter was that his brother had come down to the monastery with the intention of becoming baptized. Merton found out that John Paul had no instruction and went about preparing his brother for baptism. He gave him a large number of books, including The Imitation of Christ, the Bible, the Catechism of the Council of Trent, and Thérèse of Lisieux's autobiography, The Story of a Soul, and instructed him over the course of several days. After this instruction, John Paul was baptized at a local parish.

Thereafter, Thomas and John Paul kept up correspondence. Merton learned that his brother had married and was to be stationed overseas. One day, he received a telegram that his brother was missing in action. Eventually, Merton learned that John Paul had died in a plane crash over the Atlantic Ocean.

Merton was now the only family member in his immediate family who was still alive. He grew accustomed to the way of life of the Trappists, which included great periods of silence, manual labor, study, penance, and liturgy. Nestled in the hills of Kentucky, the Trappist monastery of Gethsemani was peaceful beyond anything that Merton could have hoped for. He began to see that his life and the life of every monk is actually a sign of the Kingdom of God to those in the world. In fact, the title of a book that he wrote five years after entering the monastery is entitled The Sign of Jonas. What did he mean by this enigmatic title? Merton explains:

> The sign Jesus promised to the generations that did not understand Him was the "sign of Jonas the prophet"— that is, the sign of His own resurrection. The life of every monk, of every priest, of every Christian is signed with the sign of Jonas, because we all live by the power of Christ's resurrection. But I feel that my own life is especially sealed with this great sign, which baptism and monastic profession and priestly ordination have burned into the roots of my being, because like Jonas himself I find myself traveling toward my destiny in the belly of a paradox. (Sign of Jonas, 7)

Merton made his solemn vows on March 19, 1947. Shortly after this, The Seven Storey Mountain, Merton's autobiography, was published. Although it might seem impertinent for a young man to write an autobiography, it might have been the case that he was ordered to write it under obedience. No one expected the book to be a national sensation, except perhaps for Merton, who had an inkling that it would be popular, but not necessarily a great work of literature.

When the time came for him to be ordained to the priesthood, he greeted it joyfully, remarking that he had been born for that moment. On May 26, 1949, Merton was ordained to the priesthood and said his first Mass. In looking back, he saw his ordination as the culmination of his seven-year spiritual journey at Gethsemani. Although this was the apex of his spiritual journey up to that point, it marked only the beginning of his life as a Catholic priest. A vocation and the priesthood, however, are forever. Would Merton remain satisfied in his situation, or would he lose his first fervor?.

Restlessness

At first, Merton was content with his new life as a Trappist priest. He was appointed Master of Scholastics in 1951. It was the role of the Master of Scholastics to train and educate students, i.e. those who were preparing for temporary vows. In this capacity, Merton gave lectures and conferences and taught his students. Merton seemed to enjoy his new life, but something beneath his superficial appearance of happiness was troubling him.

Several years after his ordination, Merton became restless. It was now 1955, and Merton realized that he wanted something more in his spiritual life. Merton was doing a lot of research about the lives of the saints, in particular the Desert Fathers. It might have been in this context that he became drawn to the desert spirituality of the Camaldolese, a Benedictine offshoot founded by St. Romuald in the eleventh century that encouraged the eremitical life. Merton contemplated leaving the Trappists to join the Camaldolese. He was getting tired of the interpersonal conflicts that occasionally occurred in the monastery and yearned for virtually complete solitude.

When Merton brought up the idea of his transferal to the Camaldolese hermits, his abbot, Dom James Fox, opposed him, but appeared to extend an olive branch to Merton by promising him that he would mention the idea of Merton becoming a hermit in the Gethsemani forest to the Trappists who were in authority over Fox. Merton was hopeful, but his hope was to be unfounded. Dom Gabriel Sortais rejected this idea. Furthermore, it was decided that Merton would become the Master of Novices, which meant that he was even more closely associated with the monastery than ever and placed in a position in which he would be forced to be in contact with other Trappists.

Merton seemed to be constantly frustrated with Dom James Fox, a graduate of Harvard Business School. Fox's style as an abbot was characterized by organizational skill and conventionalism, which went against Merton's innate desire to explore. Under Fox's leadership, Gethsemani had materially grown by leaps and bounds; yet, Merton described Fox's attempt to expand Gethsemani's success as an effort to make it into a kind of corporation, and in Merton's estimation, this material success was actually a sign of the abbey's failure. In Merton's view, the abbey should be focused on spiritual success, not material success.

In 1960 the Trappists at Gethsemani built a small hermitage so that they could dialogue with academics and Protestant clergy, but Merton was allowed to use it from time to time, which meant that he was allowed some of the solitude that he craved so earnestly. Merton was pleased by this move and took advantage of his time alone to read, write, and meditate. However, Merton was not placated completely, since he still had to endure censorship. According to Sortais, a monk should be a somewhat anonymous figure and should not express his theological opinions publically. This was not possible in Merton's case since the publication of The Seven Storey Mountain had made him something of a celebrity. The very concept of a celebrity-monk seems to be something of an oxymoron. Nevertheless, this was Merton's position, and his intellectual gifts made it imperative for him to write. When his writing seemed to challenge the status quo with the ecclesiastical authorities, it raised red flags in the minds of Merton's superiors.

Even before the conflict surfaced, there were some inklings that Merton's views were becoming more progressive. This was the Fifties, however, when prominent progressives included the likes of Pierre Teilhard de Chardin, Henri de Lubac, and Joseph Ratzinger (Benedict XVI). The theological and philosophical stances of these "progressives" was only progressive in relation to the neo-scholasticism that was in vogue at the time. Any idea that seemed to threaten the eternal nature of truth, such as evolution and the development of tradition, was looked upon with grave suspicion and was often considered heresy. Merton chose G. K. Chesterton as his whipping boy. Annoyed with the neatly packaged explanations in Chesterton's writings, Merton sensed that the truth, being complex and multi-layered, eluded such facile categorization. In contrast to Chesterton's packaged account of Thomas Aquinas, Merton proposed the subtle and culturally relevant theology of Romano Guardini, a Swiss theologian who was one of Joseph Ratzinger's professors. Whereas Chesterton seemed to maintain that doctrinal matters are merely a matter of common sense, Guardini recognized some tremendously difficult problems in theology and refrained from providing simplistic solutions.

Merton and his superiors first locked horns regarding his public writings over an article Merton wrote on Pierre Teilhard de Chardin's The Divine Milieu in 1960, a year after Merton had disparaged Chesterton in favor of Guardini. Teilhard was a French Jesuit paleontologist and cosmologist who aroused the suspicion of the ecclesiastical authorities. His work was censored, and most of it was not published until after his death in 1955. Finally published, his work was enthusiastically embraced after Vatican II in the 1960s. An evolutionist, Teilhard postulated that the cosmos was evolving on its way to what he called the "Omega point," a superconscious state in which the man-monads would be united in the cosmic Christ. Because of the Vatican's suspicion of Teilhard, Sortais ordered Merton not to publish the article on Teilhard's work. Merton resented this order and smoldered over what he saw as Sortais's authoritarianism; nevertheless, Merton acquiesced since he felt bound to keep his vow of obedience.

Merton's superiors had won this particular skirmish. Although it may seem as though Merton would have bitterly resented Fox and would no longer respect him, Merton did respect him and required his guidance. "Dom James was the necessary polarity, the defining opposite, who both contained and directed Merton's rebellion," writes Michael Higgins. Indeed, Higgins maintains that "Merton needed Dom James and this need accounts for the painful ambivalence he felt toward his abbot" (Higgins, 47). Although Merton did not appreciate Fox's authoritarianism, he respected Fox in front of others so as not to cause scandal, and even upbraided those who spoke ill of him. Instead, he used his journals as outlets for venting his frustration. Although their personalities clashed, however, Fox and Merton were always cordial with each other.

Toward the end of Merton's life, an unexpected development took place. Higgins cites Patrick Hart, Merton's secretary, as relating:

> In spite of the fact that Dom James prevented Merton from realizing his desire to be a hermit for so many years, he eventually agreed to read a paper Merton had written on the topic at a General Chapter, saw the official approval of hermit life in the Trappist tradition, granted Merton privilege to live as a hermit, and then when he retired as abbot retreated to a hermitage as well. In addition, Dom James asked Father Louis, "Louie," to be his confessor. This was a real vote of confidence in Louie; it demands great trust to be a confessor to a monk. It speaks to how Dom James trusted Merton. (Higgins, 48–49)

This shows that although there was considerable tension between these two monks, Fox and Merton respected each other. Still, Merton and his superiors frequently disagreed, and the mutual respect that burgeoned between Merton and Fox seems to have taken a long time to ripen.

A Voice Crying Out in the Wilderness

Social justice issues were always close to Merton's heart. His zeal for a more just society had impelled him to join the Communists and led him to Friendship House with Catherine Doherty. Although Merton was privileged in getting the kind of education that he received and in being able to live off of his father's inheritance, he knew that he was privileged and was genuinely concerned about the plight of others. Furthermore, he was keenly aware of what theologians call "structures of sin," which are societal structures that adversely affect the well-being of others, so he was open to the restructuring of society so as to foster justice for the underprivileged.

In the 1950s, Merton had already described his life as a paradox in a similar sense to the sign of the prophet Jonah. In the 1960s, Merton took a more active prophetic role despite, or perhaps even as the fulfillment of, his monastic vocation. Merton felt called to engage the exterior world and did not think that the opinions of a monk should be enclosed behind monastery walls, but rather should be allowed to have a place in the world. As a result, Merton inserted himself into contemporary discussions in the 1960s that revolved around war.

Merton rejected just war theory, which had been considered the standard Catholic position on martial activities. Merton was convinced that the possibility of a nuclear holocaust changed the nature of the discussion of war in a theological context, since nuclear war threatened not only particular people but also the future of humanity itself. In 1962 Merton published Original Child Bomb, a long poem that described the events surrounding the use of the first atomic bomb in terse, robotic-like phrases bereft of emotion. In addition to this poem, Merton wrote several articles on peace and just war theory. In the words of Higgins, Merton "took on the public forces committed to the war industry, the supporters keen or tepid about nuclear arms, patriotic bishops and unthinking politicians, and Catholic moralists awash in a sea of deadly caution" (Higgins, 62). As a result of his writings, Merton's superiors—pressured by American bishops—ordered him to cease publishing articles about the subject. Although Merton obeyed yet again, he expressed his frustration in his private writings, including his journals and letters.

Another issue that Merton championed was the African American civil rights movement. Merton was involved in the race issue as early as his encounter with Catherine Doherty and Friendship House. He knew firsthand the conditions in which African Americans were living since he spent time in their neighborhoods in Harlem. Merton was a friend not only of Martin Luther King Jr., but also of James Baldwin and Edlridge Cleaver. Shortly after the assassination of King in 1968, Merton read a letter sent to him from one of his friends who mused that if King had gone to a retreat at Gethsemani, he might not have been assassinated (Higgins, 66–67). In addition to his friendships with the leaders of the racial equality movement, Merton also wrote poems and tracts on behalf of African Americans. His dedication to the race issue earned Merton great esteem in the black community.

In a certain sense, Merton was a moral prophet, calling on humanity to turn from the insanity of war and potential self-destruction and to reject internecine hatred in the racial tensions that were gripping the United States. Robert Inchausti elaborates on Merton's role as a prophet:

> There's an Old Testament tradition about how one tells a true prophet from a false prophet. In the Old Testament a true prophet is usually somebody who does not bring good news... In that sense Merton meets the test... Another test of a true prophet in the Old

Testament is that he is usually hurt by his calling. He suffers from being a prophet... A third test of the true prophet is that he challenges us rather than makes us feel good about ourselves. The false prophet is somebody who tells us that we're great the way we are... In that sense Merton certainly fit the bill as a contemplative culture critic. (Atkinson, 91–92)

Unlike the cultural situation in the days of the Old Testament prophets, however, Merton's cultural situation was such that, with the advent of the nuclear age, humanity for the first time became capable of destroying itself.

Merton was, in many respects, a voice crying out in the wilderness of sin in a way that his fellow monks could not be. The roles of prophet and monk seem to be diametrically opposed, in a certain sense, because whereas the prophet cries out against injustices, monks keep silence and are hidden from the world. In Merton, however, the two roles merged on account of his sensitivity to moral issues, the fame that he achieved through The Seven Storey Mountain, and the correspondence he had with a dizzying array of important people. There are few monks throughout history who have exercised as great of a prophetic role as Merton..

Solitude and Love

Merton's quest for solitude, partially fulfilled by his request to spend time on occasion in the hermitage that the monastery had set up, reached a climax in 1965 when he was given permission to be a full-time hermit. He immersed himself in nature when the weather was pleasant, and when it was inclement, he would say the Divine Office in his hermitage. He communed with the flowers, the trees, the birds, and the other animals. With his naturalistic tendencies, his aesthetic sensitivities, and his poetic affinities, Merton found himself in a world that he deeply appreciated. Merton was convinced that he had found what he was looking for, or at least this is what it seemed at first.

There are some indications that Merton was not completely happy with his life as a hermit. When Merton left for the hermitage, he began to think that the other Trappists had turned their backs on him. In addition to this, Merton still could not quite get away from it all since he was still a very public figure: he had publishing obligations and was—in spite of his status as a hermit—an author with contracts to fulfill. This is not to say that he did not enjoy writing, but rather that he did not merely have leisure time and no duties. Most importantly, Merton genuinely loved people and needed the support that he was able to receive from them. Aristotle describes human beings as social animals because they need society; his conclusion was that the only person who could live cut off from the rest of society was either a beast or a god, but not a man. Merton needed human association to maintain his humanity.

In March 1966, Merton met a nurse in a Louisville hospital whom he identifies in his journals as "M." This meeting was to be the beginning of a relationship that would change Merton's life. Merton was in the hospital for back surgery. After the operation had been performed, Merton was delighted to discover that he no longer felt pain when he laid down on his back. A few days after the operation, a nurse came in who announced that she had been assigned to be Merton's nurse and told him to get ready for a sponge bath. Merton eventually became drawn to her, and the two soon became enrapt in each other.

The abbot knew that there was the possibility of one of the monks falling in love with one of the nurses whenever they went to the hospital, but his expectation was that once the monk returned to the abbey, that was to be the end of the relationship. In Merton's case however, he brought his relationship with him into the monastery. He contacted her by telephone, and the two of them corresponded. Merton and M. met several times. In May, there were a couple of days when the two of them were able to go to a secluded area "where they loved ecstatically, totally, although, as he confided in his diary, there was no sexual consummation" (Higgins, 79). What this means exactly is left to the imagination of the reader. It indicates, however, that the two of them had a kind of sexual relationship.

How to interpret these episodes? It seems as though Merton was a monk who was playing with fire, a religious who was pushing the envelope and jeopardizing his vow. He sensed the gravity of his situation even if he was infatuated, but the way he interpreted these events is that this affair, as Merton called it, was actually something that was good and natural. Naturally, this interpretation is open to debate. He was open about his relationship with her with his confessor, and he eventually made a firm resolve that his monastic vow of celibacy took precedence to a relationship with M.; thus, he ended their relationship. From this standpoint, Merton is to be commended in comparison to other, notorious monks throughout history who have utterly rejected their vows of celibacy, such as Peter Abelard. Merton presumably repented and embraced his religious vows, and did not abandon himself completely to M. Perhaps the greatest damage that this episode effected was the credibility of Merton in the minds of many Catholics as a spiritual leader and a holy man, although knowledge of this episode only became public many years after his death. What, then, was the good that Merton saw in his relationship with M.?

Merton was a man who had sexual escapades as a young man, but in his view, he did not really love his girlfriends in the way that he should have. He was not cooperating with a more natural kind of love-making—the kind of love-making that he experienced with M., in which the physical love ripened into something grand. This, in Merton's view, was the beneficial aspect of the affair: it showed him how to love and how to be loved.

What did James Fox have to say about this episode in Merton's life? According to Anthony Padovino, "[Fox] said, '[Merton] fell in love. Those things happen. And then he continued with his monastic life'... [Fox] didn't see the relationship as a failure" (Atkinson, 159).

Was Merton wise in allowing this relationship to happen? No. Is it impossible for something good to occur out of something that is morally dubious or evil? No. God is able to bring about good from bad things. Is Merton to be condemned? The act itself of a monk having an affair with a woman, even if they do not reach the point of consummation, is morally wrong; at the same time, judgment of Merton's soul is God's prerogative alone. What we do know is that in November 1966, Merton ended his relationship with M. If David could commit adultery but God could still forgive him afterwards, then it is not preposterous to think that something similar happened in the case of Merton's affair with M.

Dialogue with the East and Departure

The question has come up of whether Merton compromised his Catholicism. In the opinion of Bonnie Thurston, he "would have stopped exploring other traditions if he had felt he was compromising his basic life direction" (Atkinson, 132). Robert Inchausti concurs, noting that while Merton did not think that all religions are equal paths toward God, he was convinced that "it was very important to engage other religious thinkers on their deepest conceptions of reality" (Atkinson, 135). Merton was not a religious pluralist or relativist, since he did not believe that all religious are equally valid paths to God. Instead, Merton's stance prefigured the view of Vatican II, which declares that non-Christian religions contain elements of the truth. To some, Merton's humble posture of learning from non-Christians meant that he was demeaning Catholicism, which claims to have the fullness of the truth, but Merton did not see it this way. Even the Church does not maintain that it has the fullness of the truth in the sense that it knows the fullness of the truth now; instead, it holds that the fullness of truth is implicitly present in the deposit of revelation given to it by Jesus Christ.

Why was Merton so interested in the East? There are a number of reasons. First of all, Merton was convinced that there was something awry about the Western notion of reason, with its categories and tendency toward power and domination. The East knew that "reason's summit is paradox" (Higgins, 95). Theology is not able to explain the fullness of reality since the fullness of reality is far beyond the human mind, and in this sense, apophatic theology is important. Furthermore, Merton was convinced that it was important for educated people to be familiar with Eastern literature, which had a worldview that could serve to correct some of the tendencies of the Western worldview.

Merton's interest in the East was reinvigorated when the monastery elected another abbot on January 13, 1968— Flavian Burns, who had been one of Merton's novices. Whereas James Fox liked to keep a short leash on Merton, Burns gave Merton a lot of latitude and permitted him to leave the monastery quite frequently. Except for a few occasional trips outside of the monastery, Merton had been there for about twenty-seven years. Now, as Higgins notes, "He was about to make up for lost time" (Higgins, 96).

First, Merton made his way around the United States. He visited a number of monasteries, in particular, the Monastery of Christ in the Desert in New Mexico, and travelled to Alaska and California. On the Feast of St. Teresa of Avila, October 15,

1968, Merton flew to Asia from San Francisco as a response to an invitation to give a speech at a meeting of monks in Bangkok. Before arriving in Bangkok, Merton sought spiritual gurus at different stops during his Asian tour. These included Calcutta, New Delhi, Dharamsala (where he met the Dalai Lama), Madras, Sri Lanka, Polonnaruwa, Singapore, and finally Bangkok. This itinerary enabled Merton to drink his fill of Eastern mysticism and to have conversations with eminent mystics. This was important for Merton since it is one thing to read a book and another to converse with its author: when one asks a book a question, it does not respond. There is also a difference between written tradition and lived tradition since it is often the case that more can be learned from living with someone than by reading what they have written. This was true of the world's great thinkers and religious leaders, including Socrates, Jesus, and Buddha, none of whom left any writings but instead left their lives as a witness to the shape of ultimate reality.

On December 10, Merton gave a speech entitled "Marxism and Monastic Perspectives." After presenting his paper, he said, "So, I will disappear from view and we can all have a Coke or something." Merton went to his room, where he took a shower. After this, still not quite dry, he grasped a defective standing fan which sent 220 volts of direct current through his body. Merton was given the last anointing, and his death was investigated by the Thai police, but they did not perform an autopsy. There is a general consensus that Merton's death was in fact an accident, and not a suicide or a murder.

Merton's death shocked the world. Ironically, his body was returned to the United States by a U.S. Army jet on its way back from Vietnam. Preparations were made for Merton's funeral, but his body did not arrive quite in time. As some have put it, Merton was late to his own funeral. After the funeral, Merton's grave was marked by a simple cross that is common to all of the Trappists who are buried there. And so it was that Merton came to his final resting place after years of restlessness and an ardent searching for God.

Conclusion

To ask about Merton's legacy is to ask the wrong question. It is not what Merton left behind that is important, but what and who he was that matters. Who was Merton? Simply put, he was a paradox. The man who was born into a family of artistic vagabonds who eventually struck financial security, the polyglot who could write novels as a child in a language that was not his mother tongue, the world traveler who meandered through Europe and Asia, was eventually granted permission to become a hermit on a full-time basis, to acquire the solitude that he so desperately desired. At the same time, he could not do entirely without human interaction. So it was that his affair with M. highlighted his need for human community and simultaneously threatened the basis of his monastic vocation and everything that he stood for. Merton's life was one giant paradox, and perhaps a paradox is precisely the sign that the world needs.

Although he was no a theologian, his writings convey deep theological truths. This is itself another paradox. One of the truths Merton comes across is that human reason has its limitations. This does not mean that Merton disparaged human reason and despaired of the human capacity to know the truth. Rather, what it means is that in Merton's view, it is necessary to rise above reason to acquire an experience of the

God who cannot be comprehended by human reason, but only by love. Traditional Western theology, with Thomas Aquinas as its exemplar, finds it difficult to grasp this; however, even Thomas Aquinas had a vision of God after which he ceased to write since, he relates, after this experience everything that he was writing seemed to be like straw. Merton seems to have arrived at a similar conclusion.

Merton's theological transformation is characterized by his initially voracious reading of Aquinas's Summa Theologica to his adoption of elements of Zen Buddhism. Again, this was not a compromising of Merton's faith, and he did not believe that Buddhism was necessary to complete his Christianity; what it means, however, is that there is an ultimate reality to which all of the religions are related. For Merton, God was everything, and in a certain sense, God transcends all attempts at categorization. One religious scholar characterizes Merton as:

> Someone who moved from being a very narrow, exclusive Roman Catholic believer to a wide ecumenism then on to Zen and the value of Eastern faiths, someone of integrity who moved beyond the boundaries defined by his own original faith... This

scared everybody around him because they thought they were losing him, that he was becoming transreligious or panreligious when actually he was just centering. It's like the spoke of a wheel: as we center we become closer to the core of all the other religions because the core is the same. (Higgins, 105, citing Jacques Goulet)

Another paradox in Merton's life is that although he was a deep thinker, he was also an activist, even as a Trappist monk. His tendency toward activism was evident from an early age, when he attended Communist meetings at Columbia. When his thought developed, he was able to recognize the bankruptcy and inherent problems in Communism, and he was instead able to set his sights on race relations and peace in a nuclear age.

In an address to Congress on September 24, 2015, Pope Francis praised Abraham Lincoln, Martin Luther King Jr., Dorothy Day, and Thomas Merton as four Americans who helped to bring peace to America. This shows the wide appeal that Merton has had in the world and is perhaps indicative of a burgeoning openness to Merton's thought in the upper echelons of the Catholic Church. During his own life, his superiors, partly inspired by the views of the Vatican, attempted to silence him on the issue of peace; yet, over half a century later, Merton was praised by the pope.

If one were pressed to come up with important lessons to be learned from Merton's life, they might list the following: (1) God is greater than any specific categorization into which humanity attempts to fit him; (2) even when one has gone astray, it is important to be faithful to one's vows and to turn to God; (3) seeking fulfillment in God should be a guiding principle and the highest priority in life; and (4) human beings are always individuals on a journey, and it is important for them to be aware of their divine destination. These lessons, however, do not exhaust the possible lessons one could learn from studying the life of Merton, who was simultaneously a champion of humanity and an advocate for God. In an age that extols technology and efficiency and tends to squeeze the leisure out of human beings, Merton's message of the need for silence, solitude, communion, and the quest for the divine stands like an oasis in the desert.

Recommended Reading

Atkinson, Morgan C. and Jonathan Montaldo, eds. *Soul Searching: The Journey of Thomas Merton.* Collegeville, MN: Liturgical Press, 2008.

Hart, Patrick, ed. *The Legacy of Thomas Merton.* Cistercian Fathers Series, 92. Kalamazoo, MI: Cistercian Publications, 1986.

Higgins, Michael W. Thomas *Merton: Faithful Visionary.* Collegeville, MN: Liturgical Press, 2014.

Merton, Thomas. *The Secular Journal of Thomas Merton.* New York: Dell, 1959.

———. *The Seven Storey Mountain.* New York: The New American Library, 1961.

———. *The Sign of Jonas.* Garden City, NY: Image Books, 1956.

O'Connell, Patrick F., ed. *The Vision of Thomas Merton.* Notre Dame, IN: Ave Maria Press, 2003.

Wild, Robert A., ed. *Compassionate Fire: The Letters of Thomas Merton and Catherine de Hueck Doherty*. Notre Dame, IN: Ave Maria Press, 2009.

Please enjoy the first two chapters of Pope Francis: Pastor of Mercy, written by Michael J. Ruszala, as available from Wyatt North Publishing.

Pope Francis: Pastor of Mercy

Chapter 1

There is something about Pope Francis that captivates and delights people, even people who hardly know anything about him. He was elected in only two days of the conclave, yet many who tried their hand at speculating on who the next pope might be barely included him on their lists. The evening of Wednesday, March 13, 2013, the traditional white smoke poured out from the chimney of the Sistine Chapel and spread throughout the world by way of television, Internet, radio, and social media, signaling the beginning of a new papacy.

As the light of day waned from the Eternal City, some 150,000 people gathered watching intently for any movement behind the curtained door to the loggia of St. Peter's. A little after 8:00 p.m., the doors swung open and Cardinal Tauran emerged to pronounce the traditional and joyous Latin formula to introduce the new Bishop of Rome: "Annuncio vobis gaudium magnum; habemus papam!" ("I announce to you a great joy: we have a pope!") He then announced the new Holy Father's identity: "Cardinalem Bergoglio..."

The name Bergoglio, stirred up confusion among most of the faithful who flooded the square that were even more clueless than the television announcers were, who scrambled to figure out who exactly the new pope was. Pausing briefly, Cardinal

Tauran continued by announcing the name of the new pope: "...qui sibi nomen imposuit Franciscum" ("who takes for himself the name Francis"). Whoever this man may be, his name choice resonated with all, and the crowd erupted with jubilant cheers. A few moments passed before the television announcers and their support teams informed their global audiences that the man who was about to walk onto the loggia dressed in white was Cardinal Jorge Mario Bergoglio, age 76, of Buenos Aires, Argentina.

To add to the bewilderment and kindling curiosity, when the new pope stepped out to the thunderous applause of the crowd in St. Peter's Square, he did not give the expected papal gesture of outstretched arms. Instead, he gave only a simple and modest wave. Also, before giving his first apostolic blessing, he bowed asking the faithful, from the least to the greatest, to silently pray for him. These acts were only the beginning of many more words and gestures, such as taking a seat on the bus with the cardinals, refusing a popemobile with bulletproof glass, and paying his own hotel bill after his election, that would raise eyebrows among some familiar with papal customs and delight the masses.

Is he making a pointed critique of previous pontificates? Is he simply posturing a persona to the world at large to make a point? The study of the life of Jorge Mario Bergoglio gives a clear answer, and the answer is no. This is simply who he is as a man and as a priest. The example of his thought- provoking gestures flows from his character, his life experiences, his religious vocation, and his spirituality. This book uncovers the life of the 266th Bishop of Rome, Jorge Mario Bergoglio, also known as Father Jorge, a name he preferred even while he was an archbishop and cardinal.

What exactly do people find so attractive about Pope Francis? Aldo Cagnoli, a layman who developed a friendship with the Pope when he was serving as a cardinal, shares the following: "The greatness of the man, in my humble opinion lies not in building walls or seeking refuge behind his wisdom and office, but rather in dealing with everyone judiciously, respectfully, and with humility, being willing to learn at any moment of life; that is what Father Bergoglio means to me" (as quoted in Ch. 12 of Pope Francis: Conversations with Jorge Bergoglio, previously published as El Jesuita [The Jesuit]).

At World Youth Day 2013, in Rio de Janeiro, Brazil, three million young people came out to celebrate their faith with

Pope Francis. Doug Barry, from EWTN's Life on the Rock, interviewed youth at the event on what features stood out to them about Pope Francis. The young people seemed most touched by his authenticity. One young woman from St. Louis said, "He really knows his audience. He doesn't just say things to say things... And he is really sincere and genuine in all that he does." A friend agreed: "He was looking out into the crowd and it felt like he was looking at each one of us...." A young man from Canada weighed in: "You can actually relate to [him]... for example, last night he was talking about the World Cup and athletes." A young woman added, "I feel he means what he says... he practices what he preaches... he states that he's there for the poor and he actually means it."

The Holy Spirit guided the College of Cardinals in its election of Pope Francis to meet the needs of the Church following the historic resignation of Pope Benedict XVI due to old age. Representing the growth and demographic shift in the Church throughout the world and especially in the Southern Hemisphere, Pope Francis is the first non-European pope in almost 1,300 years. He is also the first Jesuit pope. Pope Francis comes with a different background and set of experiences. Both as archbishop and as pope, his flock knows him for his humility, ascetic frugality in solidarity with the poor, and closeness. He was born in Buenos Aires to a family of Italian immigrants, earned a diploma in chemistry, and followed a priestly vocation in the Jesuit order after an experience of God's mercy while receiving the sacrament of Reconciliation. Even though he is known for his smile and humor, the world also recognizes Pope Francis as a stern figure that stands against the evils of the world and challenges powerful government officials, when necessary.

The Church he leads is one that has been burdened in the West by the aftermath of sex abuse scandals and increased secularism. It is also a Church that is experiencing shifting in numbers out of the West and is being challenged with religious persecution in the Middle East, Asia, and Africa. The Vatican that Pope Francis has inherited is plagued by cronyism and scandal. This Holy Father knows, however, that his job is not merely about numbers, politics, or even success. He steers clear of pessimism knowing that he is the head of Christ's Body on earth and works with Christ's grace. This is the man God has chosen in these times to lead his flock.

Chapter 2: Early Life in Argentina

Jorge Mario Bergoglio was born on December 17, 1936, in the Flores district of Buenos Aires. The district was a countryside locale outside the main city during the nineteenth century and many rich people in its early days called this place home. By the time Jorge was born, Flores was incorporated into the city of Buenos Aires and became a middle class neighborhood. Flores is also the home of the beautiful Romantic-styled Basilica of San José de Flores, built in 1831, with its dome over the altar, spire over the entrance, and columns at its facade. It was the Bergoglios' parish church and had much significance in Jorge's life.

Jorge's father's family had arrived in Argentina in 1929, immigrating from Piedimonte in northern Italy. They were not the only ones immigrating to the country. In the late nineteenth century, Argentina became industrialized and the government promoted immigration from Europe. During that time, the land prospered and Buenos Aires earned the moniker "Paris of the South." In the late nineteenth and early twentieth centuries waves of immigrants from Italy, Spain, and other European countries came off ships in the port of Buenos Aires. Three of Jorge's great uncles were the first in the family to immigrate to Argentina in 1922 searching for better employment opportunities after World War I. They established a paving company in Buenos Aires and built a four-story building for their company with the city's first elevator. Jorge's father and paternal grandparents followed the brothers in order to keep the family together and to escape Mussolini's fascist regime in Italy. Jorge's father and grandfather also helped with the business for a time. His father, Mario, who had been an accountant for a rail company in Italy, provided similar services for the family business (Cardinal Bergoglio recalls more on the story of his family's immigration and his early life in Ch. 1 of Conversations with Jorge Bergoglio).

Providentially, the Bergoglios were long delayed in liquidating their assets in Italy; this forced them to miss the ship they planned to sail on, the doomed Pricipessa Mafalda, which sank off the northern coast of Brazil before reaching Buenos Aires. The family took the Giulio Cesare instead and arrived safely in Argentina with Jorge's Grandma Rosa. Grandma Rosa wore a fur coat stuffed with the money the family brought with them from Italy. Economic hard times eventually hit Argentina in 1932 and the family's paving business went under, but the Bergoglio brothers began anew.

Jorge's father, Mario, met his mother Regina at Mass in 1934. Regina was born in Argentina, but her parents were also Italian immigrants. Mario and Regina married the following year after meeting. Jorge, the eldest of their five children, was born in 1936. Jorge fondly recalls his mother gathering the children around the radio on Sunday afternoons to listen to opera and explain the story. A true porteño, as the inhabitants of the port city of Buenos Aires are called, Jorge liked to play soccer, listen to Latin music, and dance the tango. Jorge's paternal grandparents lived around the corner from his home. He greatly admired his Grandma Rosa, and keeps her written prayer for her grandchildren with him until this day. Jorge recalls that while his grandparents kept their personal conversations in Piedmontese, Mario chose mostly to speak Spanish, preferring to look forward rather than back. Still, Jorge grew up speaking both Italian and Spanish.

Upon entering secondary school at the age of thirteen, his father insisted that Jorge begin work even though the family, in their modest lifestyle, was not particularly in need of extra income. Mario Bergoglio wanted to teach the boy the value of work and found several jobs for him during his adolescent years. Jorge worked in a hosiery factory for several years as a cleaner and at a desk. When he entered technical school to study food chemistry, Jorge found a job working in a laboratory. He worked under a woman who always challenged him to do his work thoroughly. He remembers her, though, with both fondness and sorrow. Years later, she was kidnapped and murdered along with members of her family because of her political views during the Dirty War, a conflict in the 1970's and 80's between the military dictatorship and guerrilla fighters in which thousands of Argentineans disappeared.

Initially unhappy with his father's decision to make him work, Jorge recalls later in his life that work was a valuable formative experience for him that taught him responsibility, realism, and how the world operated. He learned that a person's self worth often comes from their work, which led him to become committed later in life to promote a just culture of work rather than simply encouraging charity or entitlement. He believes that people need meaningful work in order to thrive. During his boyhood through his priestly ministry, he experienced the gulf in Argentina between the poor and the well off, which left the poor having few opportunities for gainful employment.

At the age of twenty-one, Jorge became dangerously ill. He was diagnosed with severe pneumonia and cysts. Part of his upper right lung was removed, and each day Jorge endured the pain and discomfort of saline fluid pumped through his chest to clear his system. Jorge remembers that the only person that was able to comfort him during this time was a religious sister who had catechized him from childhood, Sister Dolores. She exposed him to the true meaning of suffering with this simple statement: "You are imitating Christ." This stuck with him, and his sufferings during that time served as a crucible for his character, teaching him how to distinguish what is important in life from what is not. He was being prepared for what God was calling him to do in life, his vocation.

16854175R00075

Made in the USA
Middletown, DE
25 November 2018